Letter to Santa

Dear Santa,

My name is_____ I am_____ years old.

I live in _____

This year i have been:

□ Very good   □ Mostly good   □ A little Naughty

Some special Christmas wishes I have are:

_____

_____

_____

Some other things I'd like if you have room in your Sleigh:

_____

_____

_____

From your friend,_____

Letter to Santa

Dear Santa,

My name is _____ I am _____ years old.

I live in _____

This year i have been:

☐ Very good   ☐ Mostly good   ☐ A little Naughty

Some special Christmas wishes I have are:

_____

_____

_____

Some other things I'd like if you have room in your Sleigh:

_____

_____

_____

From your friend, _____

Letter to Santa

Dear Santa,

My name is _____ I am _____ years old.

I live in _____

This year i have been:

☐ Very good   ☐ Mostly good   ☐ A little Naughty

Some special Christmas wishes I have are:

_____

_____

_____

Some other things I'd like if you have room in your Sleigh:

_____

_____

_____

From your friend, _____

Letter to Santa

Dear Santa,

My name is _____ I am _____ years old.

I live in _____

This year i have been:

☐ Very good   ☐ Mostly good   ☐ A little Naughty

Some special Christmas wishes I have are:

_____

_____

_____

Some other things I'd like if you have room in your Sleigh:

_____

_____

_____

From your friend,_____

Letter to Santa

Dear Santa,

My name is _____ I am _____ years old.

I live in _____

This year i have been:

☐ Very good   ☐ Mostly good   ☐ A little Naughty

Some special Christmas wishes I have are:

_____

_____

_____

Some other things I'd like if you have room in your Sleigh:

_____

_____

_____

From your friend, _____

Letter to Santa

Dear Santa,

My name is _____ I am _____ years old.

I live in _____

This year i have been:

☐ Very good   ☐ Mostly good   ☐ A little Naughty

Some special Christmas wishes I have are:

_____

_____

_____

Some other things I'd like if you have room in your Sleigh:

_____

_____

_____

From your friend, _____

Letter to Santa

Dear Santa,

My name is _____ I am _____ years old.

I live in _____

This year i have been:

☐ Very good   ☐ Mostly good   ☐ A little Naughty

Some special Christmas wishes I have are:

_____
_____
_____

Some other things I'd like if you have room in your Sleigh:

_____
_____
_____

From your friend,_____

From:

From:

From:

From:

From:

From:

From:

From:

From:

From:

Made in the USA
Middletown, DE
05 December 2021